CRAFTY FUN
WITH CLAY!

25 brilliant ideas, from pretty pots to scary monsters

Thomasina Smith

ARMADILLO

This edition is published by Armadillo, an imprint of Anness Publishing Ltd,
108 Great Russell Street, London WC1B 3NA; info@anness.com

www.annesspublishing.com

If you like the images in this book and would like to investigate using them for publishing,
promotions or advertising, please visit www.practicalpictures.com for more information.

Publisher: Joanna Lorenz
Editors: Lyn Coutts, Richard McGinlay, Sophie Warne
Photographer: Tim Ridley
Designer: Michael R Carter
Production Controller: Pirong Wang

PUBLISHER'S NOTE
Although the advice and information in this book are believed to be accurate and true at the
time of going to press, neither the authors nor the publisher can accept any legal responsibility
or liability for any errors or omissions that may have been made nor for any inaccuracies nor for
any loss, harm or injury that comes about from following instructions or advice in this book.

Manufacturer: Anness Publishing Ltd, 108 Great Russell Street, London WC1B 3NA, England
For Product Tracking go to: www.annesspublishing.com/tracking
Batch: 0613-23131-1127

Introduction

Astound your friends with these weird and wonderful models! There are loads of projects to make, including peoples, animals, creepy crawlies, rockets, monsters and a pirate's treasure chest. After making a few of the models in this book, why not design some of your own? You could even write a story or a play using the characters and objects you have made.

Some of the models use drying material, which hardens in about 24 hours without baking. Others use material that has to be baked in an oven. Plastic material does not harden, so it can be reused – use this material to perfect your model-making skills. Always store your materials in airtight plastic bags in a cool, dark place and keep your chopping board and tools clean. Be creative and you are bound to have fun!

Thomasina Smith

Contents

Materials and Equipment

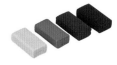
Baking material

Candles

ACRYLIC PAINT
This water-based paint is available from art and stationery stores. It comes in a range of vibrant shades. If you want to mix your own shades, use a plastic paint palette or an old plate.

BAKING MATERIAL
This kind of clay hardens when it is baked in an oven. It comes in a range of shades. Always read the instructions on the packet.

BAKING TRAY
You will need a baking tray when using baking material.

BUTTONS
Buttons are ideal for decorating and for making noses and eyes for your models.

CARDBOARD
A cardboard box is perfect for cutting up and using as a strong base for heavy models. For lighter structures, use thin cardboard, which comes in a variety of shades.

CHOPPING BOARD
A plastic chopping board will protect the tabletop while you work and will give an even surface for rolling out materials.

DOUBLE-SIDED TAPE
This tape is sticky on both sides. Use it to join cardboard together without the tape being seen.

DRYING MATERIAL
This kind of clay comes in large white or terracotta blocks. It will harden in about 24 hours without baking. Always read the instructions on the packet.

ELECTRICAL TAPE
This is a very strong adhesive tape that is available in lots of shades.

KNIFE
A knife is a very effective tool for cutting through clay.

MASKING TAPE
Use this tape to join cardboard that will be covered with clay.

Baking tray

Candle holders

Buttons

Plate

Acrylic paints

PAINTBRUSHES
If possible, buy a good quality brush because it is unlikely to shed its bristles. Have one brush for painting and another for gluing.

PASTRY CUTTER
This is used to cut interesting shapes from clay. You can use a plastic or metal pastry cutter. Wash it after you have used it.

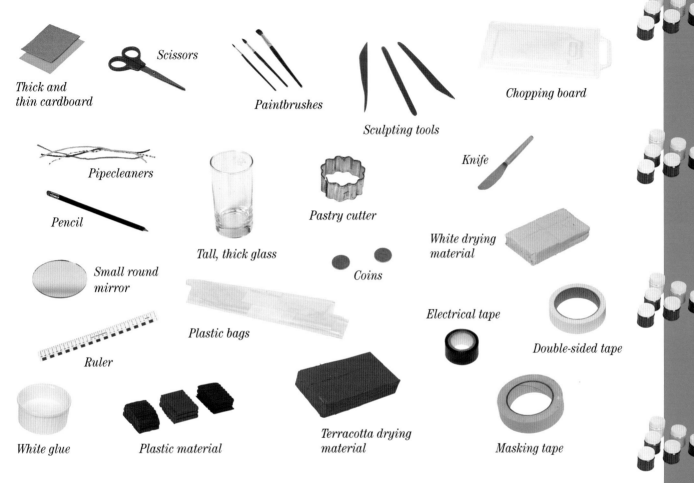

Thick and thin cardboard

Scissors

Paintbrushes

Sculpting tools

Chopping board

Pipecleaners

Knife

Pencil

Pastry cutter

Tall, thick glass

White drying material

Small round mirror

Coins

Electrical tape

Plastic bags

Double-sided tape

Ruler

White glue

Plastic material

Terracotta drying material

Masking tape

PIPECLEANERS

These come in a range of shades and can be used to decorate your models. They can be bent to make legs, arms or flower stems.

PLASTIC BAGS

A plastic bag is essential for storing drying material. Always seal the bag very tightly, to prevent the material from hardening.

PLASTIC MATERIAL

Widely known by the brand name Plasticine, this inexpensive and reusable material comes in lots of bright shades. It does not harden, so the models are less permanent.

SCULPTING TOOL

The most useful kind of tool for carving and shaping models has one pointy end and one flat end.

TALL, THICK GLASS

Use for rolling out clay and making circles. Do not use a wooden rolling pin, as the material will stick to it.

WHITE GLUE

A varnish made from 8 parts white glue (also known as PVA glue) and 1 part water will protect your models and give them a smooth, shiny finish.

Basic Techniques

STARTING OFF

To soften baking material – hold it in your hands and let their warmth soften the clay. This will make it easy to model.

KEEPING CLAY SEPARATE

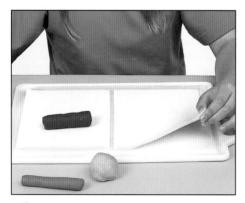

1 To stop different shades of plastic material from being mixed together, tape sheets of white paper on to your work surface or chopping board.

ROLLING MATERIALS

To roll out material – use a tall, straight, thick glass to roll out clay. Apply pressure evenly in order to get a smooth surface of the right thickness.

2 Roll or model only one shades of material on each sheet. After finishing a model, put the paper aside and use it the next time you use that shade.

SHAPING MATERIALS

To make snakes and sausages – roll the material back and forth under the palms of your hands. Move your hands along the material to make it an even width.

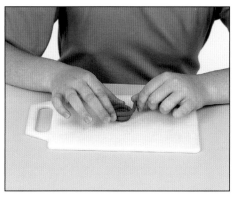

To make a coil pot – tightly coil a snake of material to make the base. Make the sides by winding layers of snakes around the outer edge.

To make a perfectly round ball – roll a piece of material vigorously between your palms. Balls of clay make excellent heads and hands.

To make a flat circle – roll a piece of material between your palms to make a ball. Place the base of a thick glass on top of the ball and press down firmly.

9

Making Patterns

1 Make patterns in clay using a metal or plastic pastry cutter. Some cutters make flowery circular patterns, others zigzag designs.

2 Press the flat side of a sculpting tool on to the material to make petal shapes for a flower or the dazzling rays of the Sun.

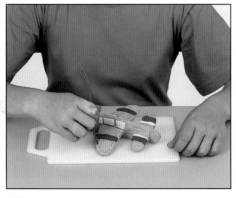

3 To decorate and add interesting details to your models, use the pointed end of a sculpting tool or paintbrush to make dents in the material.

4 Use the edge of a sculpting tool to give texture to your models. This technique is especially useful when you are making animal models.

Building Walls

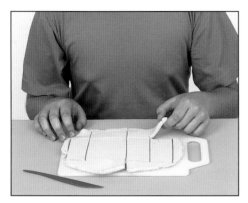

1 A popular technique in model making is to build walls using slabs of clay. First, roll out a piece of material and cut it into rectangles.

2 Score the edges of the base with fine lines. Position the first wall and use a tool to graft, or bind, them together. Position the next wall.

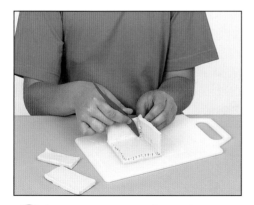

3 Support this wall with your fingers while you get the next wall into position. Always bind the joins together on the inside of the structure.

4 When all the walls are in place and the inside joins are secure, use a sculpting tool to smooth and neaten the outside seams.

Bodies

MAKING FACES

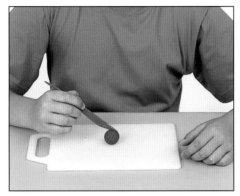

1 To make eyes, roll a small ball of material and cut it in half. Each half makes a perfect eye.

2 To make a mouth, insert the sculpting tool into the head of the model and move it from side to side. To make an open mouth, lever the tool up and down.

ATTACHING LIMBS

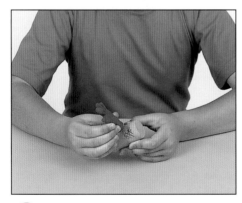

1 One way of securely fixing limbs to a body is to score lines on both pieces. Press the pieces together and bind the join using a sculpting tool.

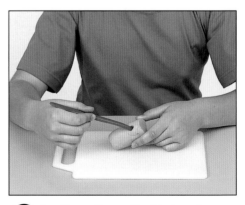

2 An alternative method is to make a hole in the body with the thin end of a sculpting tool. Shape the end of the limb into a point and fit it into the hole firmly.

Finishing Touches

DECORATIVE EXTRAS

1 An upside-down glass pressed firmly down into your material will make a perfect circle.

2 Different shapes of pastry cutters can be used to make stars, flowers, diamonds, hearts and all sorts of animals.

PAINTING AND PRESERVING MODELS

1 Drying material can be painted using acrylic or poster paints. Allow the model to dry before painting. To get a good finish, apply two coats of paint.

2 Preserve models made from drying or baking material with a solution of 8 parts white glue to 1 part water. Apply with a paintbrush on to dry models only.

13

The Big Pink Bus

All over the world people use buses. In countries such as India, Indonesia and the Philippines buses are brightly painted and passengers strap their luggage on to special racks on the top of the buses. If your school bus is a double-decker, make the model taller and add an extra row of windows. Once you have made a bus, you can go on to model lots of other different vehicles.

YOU WILL NEED

White drying material
Chopping board
Knife
Ruler
4 coins
Acrylic paints in red, yellow, blue, black, white
Paintbrush
White glue

HANDY HINT
The shades of paint and clay listed in the instructions are only suggestions. Let your imagination go wild and use the entire rainbow when making your models!

1 Use the knife to cut a rectangle of material 8cm/3in wide, 4cm/1½in high and 5cm/2in long. Cut a block 2cm/⅜in deep from one end of the rectangle to make the front of the bus.

2 Carefully carve lines on all sides of the bus for the windows. On the front of the bus, carve a radiator and two circles for the headlights. You can add more detail if you want to.

3 Press the coins into the bus to make the wheels. Cut a shallow rectangular hole in the roof to make the rack. Shape small pieces for luggage. Allow the bus to dry for about 12 hours on each side.

4 Paint the bus and the luggage with acrylic paints. When dry, glue the luggage to the roof of the bus. Allow the glue to dry before applying a varnish of 8 parts white glue diluted in 1 part water.

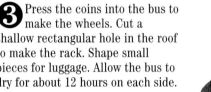

Scary Monster

Scare your friends and family with this fearsome monster. It may only have one tooth, but beware of this beast's long red tongue. You could make a family of scary monsters in different sizes and shades, then use them to act out a horror story.

YOU WILL NEED
Non-hardening plastic material
in yellow, orange, green, red,
white, black
Chopping board
Ruler
Sculpting tool

HANDY HINT
To make your monster look more
interesting, try blending two or
three shades of plastic material.
Gently roll them together on the
chopping board.

1 Use yellow material to roll a ball 3cm/1⅛in wide for the monster's head and another ball 1cm/½in wide for its nose. Then make a sausage 10cm/4in long and 4cm/1½in wide for the body.

2 Roll thin snakes in green and orange material for the hair. Shape red material into a tongue. Make two white balls and two black dots for the eyes. Use the sculpting tool to carve green arms and hands.

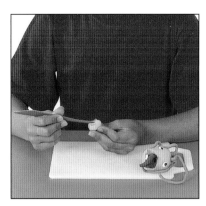

3 Make a hole in the face for the mouth. Shape white material to make a tooth and press it on to the mouth. Then position the tongue and eyes. Make small holes in the head and insert the hair. Use a pointed tool to make nostrils. Press the nose firmly into position.

4 Make a small hole in either side of the body. Shape the end of each arm to fit into each hole snugly. Make sure the arms are secure by binding the joins. Smooth rough surfaces with the tool.

5 Score lines on the top of the body and the base of the head. This will make it easier to join the pieces together. Push the head on firmly, taking care not to squash the monster's face!

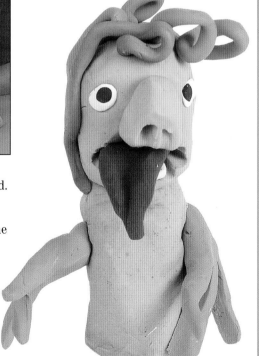

Spotty Elephant

All animal lovers will enjoy making this elephant model. It is decorated with yellow spots and a yellow bow, but flowers or stripes would be just as much fun. The tricky bit is making the trunk. Take care not to roll it too long and thin or it will droop! If you enjoyed making this model, you can go on to make the whole crazy herd.

YOU WILL NEED
Non-hardening plastic material
  in blue, orange, red, purple
Chopping board
Ruler
Tall, thick glass
Knife
Sculpting tool

1 Roll one ball 10cm/4in wide, four sausages 2cm/¾in wide and two balls 6cm/2½in wide from blue material. Roll out the largest ball to make the body. Press on the legs. Cut one ball in half and flatten to make ears.

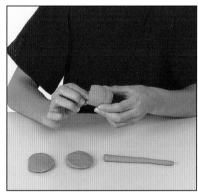

2 Shape the remaining ball to make the elephant's head and face. Roll another piece of blue material to make a ball about 3cm/1¼in wide. Shape it into a thick sausage for the trunk.

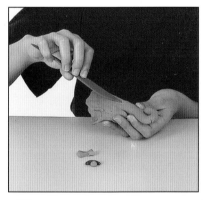

3 Press the ears and trunk on to the elephant's head and sculpt them together using the tool. Roll out a little orange material and cut a bow and two eyes from this. Add red material to the eyes to make the pupils and eyelids.

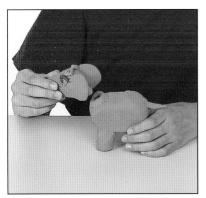

4 Press the bow and eyes on to the head. Make a hole in the body where the head will go. Shape the head to fit snugly into the hole and press it in firmly. Sculpt and smooth the join with the tool.

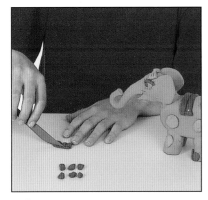

5 To make the elephant's toenails, roll 12 tiny red balls and join them together in four sets of three. Flatten with the tool before gently pressing one set to the front of each leg. Add some spots, a saddle, and finally a tail!

19

Snappy Crocodile

This fantastic crocodile is made from a special clay that hardens when baked in the oven. This means that your crocodile will be flashing its fangs at passers-by for years to come! Just like a real crocodile, this model has enormous teeth and keeps its mouth open to stay cool. Why not make a toothy crocodile as a reminder to your family to brush their teeth?

YOU WILL NEED

Baking material in green, white, red
Chopping board
Ruler
Sculpting tool
Baking tray

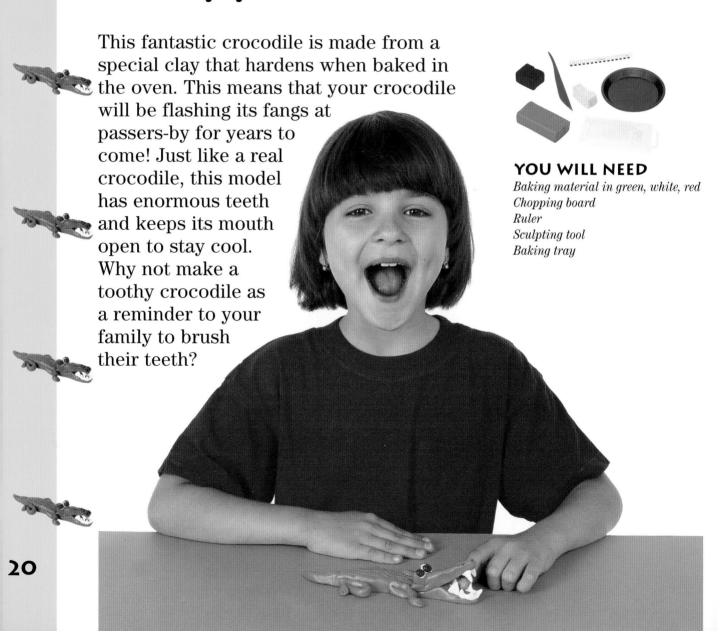

20

1 Roll one sausage 16cm/6½in long, another 6cm/2½in long and four sausages 5cm/2in long. Roll two balls for the bulging eyes. Shape the two large sausages to make the body and upper jaw.

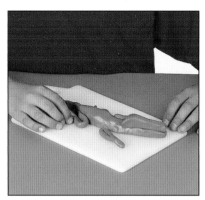

2 Press the jaw and legs into position. Bend the back legs to look like those of a real crocodile. Fold the front legs so that they are thicker at the top. Smooth the joins with your fingers.

3 Cut and stick a ball of white material on to each of the small green balls. Press a little red material on top to complete the eyes. Press on the eyes to cover the join between the jaw and body.

4 Cut four rectangular strips of white material. Carefully carve small triangles from the strips to make the crocodile's teeth. Position them neatly along the crocodile's jaws.

5 Use the sculpting tool to mark scales on the crocodile's back. Place your masterpiece on a baking tray. Ask an adult to put it in the oven and to bake it according to the instructions on the packet.

21

Fun with Fruit

This plate of clay fruit looks good enough to eat! It would make a wonderful gift for a friend or relative. Once you have mastered apples, oranges and bananas, experiment with larger or more complicated fruit like a pineapple or bunch of grapes. Remember to make the pineapple much bigger than the apple and orange.

YOU WILL NEED

Drying material
Chopping board
Tall, thick glass
Plate or bowl
Sculpting tool
Acrylic paints in white, blue, yellow, green, red
Paintbrush
White glue

HANDY HINT

An easy way to make a plate or bowl from drying material is to use a plate or bowl as a template. Line the inside of the plate or bowl with an even layer of rolled out material. When it dries and hardens, the material will shrink away from the sides.

1 Roll out a piece of drying material using the glass. The piece should be large enough to cover the plate and thick enough not to fall apart. Lift it on to the plate and trim the edges.

2 Roll two balls of material in your palms to make the apple and the orange. Roll out a thick sausage for the banana and shape the ends. Then roll out a piece of material for the banana skin.

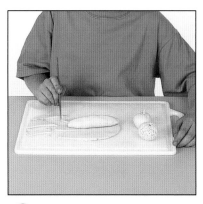

3 Pierce tiny holes in one of the balls to look like the skin of an orange. Make a dent in the top of the apple and insert a stalk. Lay the banana on the rolled out material and cut it as shown.

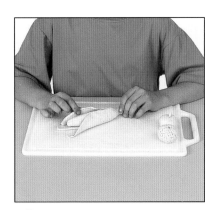

4 Wrap the skin around the banana so that the edges meet neatly and the flaps curl over. Pinch one end to form the banana stalk. Leave the plate and fruit to dry for about 12 hours on each side.

5 Paint the plate and fruit, remembering to rinse the paintbrush before switching to different paint. Allow to dry. Varnish your model with a solution of 8 parts white glue to 1 part water.

23

Space Rocket

This rocket was made using a cardboard base covered with plastic material. Not only does this method make the model stronger, but it also means that you can be more inventive when you design your own deep-space explorer.

YOU WILL NEED

Thick cardboard
Pencil
Ruler
Scissors
Masking tape
Chopping board

Non-hardening plastic material in white, black, purple, green, orange, yellow
Tall, thick glass
Sculpting tool

1 On a piece of cardboard, draw two tongue shapes 20cm/8in long and 8cm/3in wide. On one of the shapes, mark a 3mm/1in wide slit, as shown. On the other, draw semi-circular fins on either side.

2 Cut out both shapes and the slit. Slot the finned piece into the slit so that the rocket will stand upright. If the model leans to one side, trim the base to straighten it. Fasten the joins with masking tape.

3 Roll out pieces of plastic material in different shades. Press these on to the card base, pinching the joins together securely. Use the sculpting tool to trim the edges and draw markings.

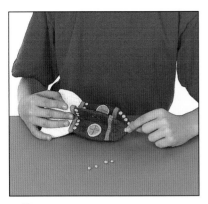

4 When the rocket is covered with clay, press on flattened balls of the material to make windows and rivets.

5 Shape an astronaut from white material. Make a hole in a window and shape the astronaut to fit snugly into the hole.

25

Ghoul and Chain

This spooky ghoul is an excellent model to give to a friend at Halloween. It is very easy to make and definitely scary! If you listen hard you might even hear the chains rattle. To make your ghoul a truly horrifying spectacle, model it in glow-in-the-dark material, which is available from art stores. Replace the plastic material chain with an old broken necklace chain if you like.

YOU WILL NEED

Non-hardening plastic material in white, purple
Chopping board
Ruler
Sculpting tool
Scissors

HANDY HINT

A great game to play with friends at Halloween is to see who can make the scariest and most gruesome spook!

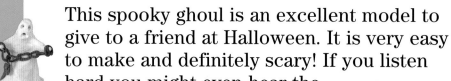

1 Roll a sausage of white plastic material to measure 8cm/3in long and 5cm/2in wide. Roll the sausage unevenly so that one end is fatter than the other. The fatter end will be the base of the ghoul.

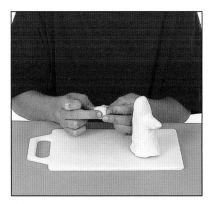

2 Sculpt the sausage into a ghost shape. Shape two pieces of white material for the arms and press them into position. Smooth the joins with your fingers or the sculpting tool.

3 Use the sculpting tool to carve eye holes and a mouth on to the face of your ghoul. This ghoul looks very sad with its down-turned mouth. You could make a friendly ghoul by giving it a smile.

4 Roll out the purple material into thin snakes. Cut into pieces about 5cm/2in long. Loop one piece into a circle, then link the next piece on to it to make a chain. Continue, and make the chain as wide as the ghoul.

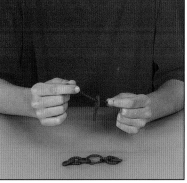

5 Cut out a key and make a small hole in it using the sculpting tool. Thread a piece of purple material through the key and link it on to the chain. Make two links to attach the chain to the ghoul's arms.

Treasure Chest

This treasure chest is a great place to keep small and precious things. It is made of drying material that slowly hardens when it is left in the air. The skull and crossbones shown on the front is the traditional sign of a pirate ship.

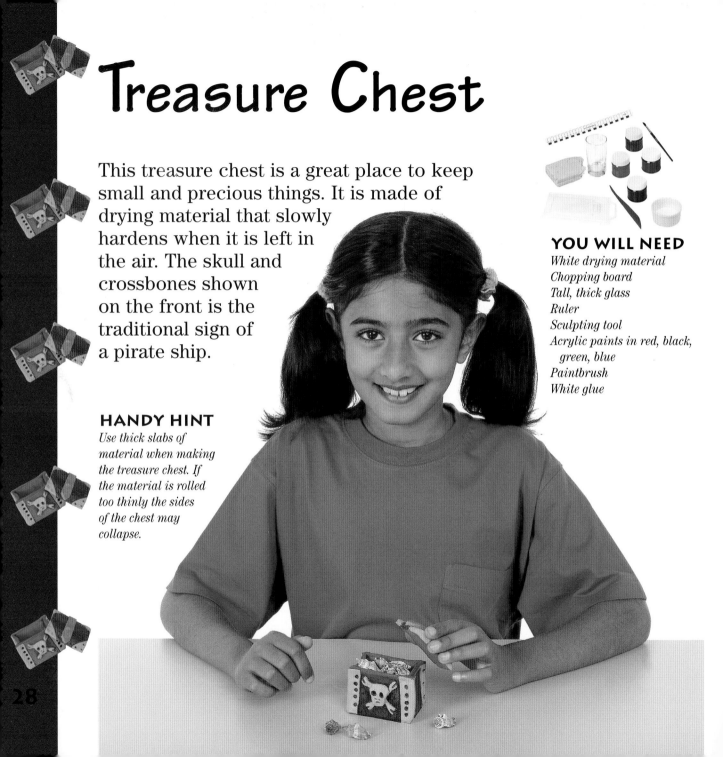

YOU WILL NEED

White drying material
Chopping board
Tall, thick glass
Ruler
Sculpting tool
Acrylic paints in red, black, green, blue
Paintbrush
White glue

HANDY HINT
Use thick slabs of material when making the treasure chest. If the material is rolled too thinly the sides of the chest may collapse.

28

1 Roll out the clay. Mark and then cut out two sides and a base each 6cm/2½in by 4cm/1½in, and two more sides each 4cm/1½in square. Also cut out a strip 8cm/3in long to make the strap for the lid.

2 Score around the sides of the base using the sculpting tool. Position the first side and smooth the inside join. Continue positioning the remaining sides and smoothing the inside joins with the tool.

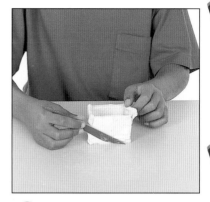

3 When all the sides are in place, smooth the outside edges with the tool. Gently support the sides as you work. Use the point of the tool to make dots in the clay to create the effect of studs.

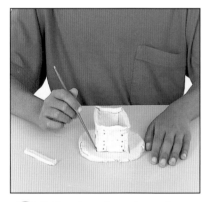

4 Roll out another piece of drying material and place the chest on it. Cut around the chest so that the rectangle for the lid will be exactly the same size as the base of the chest.

5 Decorate the lid and press the strap on to the lid. Place the lid on the chest. Decorate the chest with a skull and crossbones cut from drying material. Allow the chest to dry for 24 hours.

6 When the chest is dry and hard, paint it inside and outside with acrylic paints. Allow the paint to dry before applying a coat of varnish made from 8 parts white glue to 1 part water.

29

Queen Chess Piece

The queen is one of the most important pieces in the game of chess. She holds an orb and sceptre and wears a crown. Add an extra special touch by decorating the crown with gold and red glitter glue. If you are a keen chess player you could design and make a complete set of chess pieces.

YOU WILL NEED

Non-hardening plastic material in blue, white, red, yellow
Chopping board
Ruler
Tall, thick glass
Sculpting tool

HANDY HINT

If you would like a long-lasting model, you could make the Queen chess piece from drying material. Finish the piece by painting and then varnishing it.

1 To make the body of the queen, roll a thick sausage of blue material 13cm/5in long and 5cm/2in wide. To make the base of the chess piece, roll a ball 5cm/2in wide from the same material.

2 Roll a thin snake of the same material 14cm/5½in long. Trim both ends of the body using a sculpting tool. Flatten the ball with the bottom of the glass to form a flat round base.

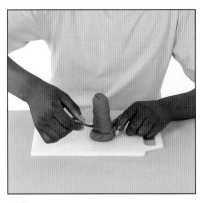

3 Roll the body unevenly so that it is thinner at one end. This will be the top. Press the fatter end on to the base. Wrap the thin snake of material around the join.

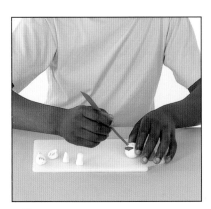

4 Clean the chopping board. Make a head, neck, two hands and a nose from white material. Make a pair of lips from red material. Press lips and nose on to the face and mark eyes with the tool. Attach the neck.

5 Make a hole on either side of the body. Shape the hands so that they will fit snugly into each hole. Press the neck and head on to the body. Add the yellow crown, orb and sceptre. Then trim with red.

Birthday Cake

What could be more fitting than to make a beautiful cake for a friend's birthday? Decorate the cake with candles and miniature models of confectionery. You could also cut your friend's initials out of clay and press them on to the cake.

YOU WILL NEED
Non-hardening plastic material
* in blue, white, orange, purple*
Chopping board
Tall, thick glass
Sculpting tool
Candles
Candle holders

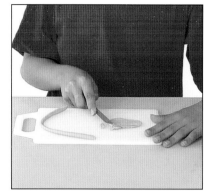

1 Use the palms of your hands to roll two balls of blue material and one ball of white material. All three balls should be the same size. Flatten each ball with the bottom of the glass and trim the edges.

2 Sandwich the white disc between the two blue discs to look like a layer of cream. Roll a thin snake and a flat circle from the orange material. Carve a bow from the circle of orange material.

3 Wrap the orange snake around the base of the cake to look like a plate. Press the bow on to the front of the cake. Shape small balls of white and purple material to make cake decorations for the top.

SAFETY NOTE
Do not light the candles on the model birthday cake. They are only for decoration. If you like, you can replace the candles with stripey straws that have been cut to the right length.

4 Put the candles in the candle holders, then push the candle holders into the top of the cake. The candles should alternate with the cake decorations. Now it is time to sing Happy Birthday!

33

Wonder Boy

Like all great superheroes, Wonder Boy wears a dashing cape and has superhuman powers. You could build a whole story world about Wonder Boy's adventures from clay. Your hero could save a city of skyscrapers from rampaging monsters and dinosaurs elsewhere in the book!

YOU WILL NEED
*Non-hardening plastic material in
   green, orange, white, red, yellow
Chopping board
Sculpting tool*

1 Roll out four small sausages and one large sausage from green material. The large sausage will be the superhero's body, so it should be narrow at the top and wide at the bottom.

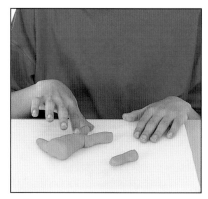

2 Firmly press the four small sausages on to the body to make the legs and arms of Wonder Boy. Use your fingers to carefully bind and smooth the joins. Make sure that your model can stand.

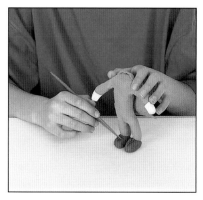

3 Roll out orange material and shape it to make a cloak. Shape two white balls to make fists, and two red balls to make a pair of chunky shoes. Press the pieces into position and decorate.

4 To make Wonder Boy's face, roll a ball of white material. Use scraps of the other shades of material to make the eyes, mouth and nose. Carve a piece of yellow material for the hair and press it into position.

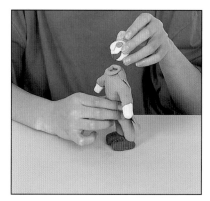

5 Roll a thin sausage of green material, shape it into a small circle and position it where Wonder Boy's head will go. Press the head firmly on to the body and smooth the join. Lay the model down gently on its back.

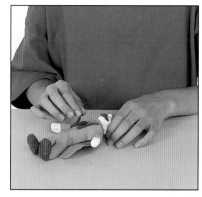

6 Roll out a thin snake of red material. Place it on Wonder Boy's chest in the shape of the letter 'W'. Press it firmly into position. If your superhero has a different name, make the appropriate initial.

Piglet Badge

This badge is made from baking material, which hardens when baked in the oven. This piglet is wearing a smart suit and tie, but you could dress your piggy in shorts, a T-shirt and cool sunglasses if you prefer! In fact, why not make a menagerie of well-dressed animals?

YOU WILL NEED

Baking material in green, light or dark pink, red
Chopping board
Ruler
Sculpting tool
Baking tray
Safety pin
Electrical tape

HANDY HINT

It is easier to make shapes with baking material if it is warmed in your hands first. Some shades tend to be easier to work with than others, so it is worth experimenting.

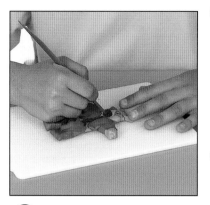

1 In green, cut three rectangles 1cm/½in by 2cm/1in for the legs, four 1cm/½in squares for the coat and two tiny pieces for eyes. In pink, cut two rectangles 1cm/½in by 2cm/1in for the body and head, two small pieces for ears and two pieces for hands.

2 Warm the pieces in your hands before shaping each one with your fingers. Lay out the pieces in the correct position and press them together with your fingers. Mark the eyes with the sculpting tool.

3 Decorate the piglet with a tie and buttons. Shape a snout and make the nostrils. Press on the snout. Place the piglet on the baking tray. Ask an adult to bake it following the packet instructions.

4 Leave the model to cool thoroughly. Fix the safety pin on to the back of the piglet with strong electrical tape.

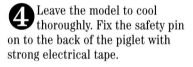

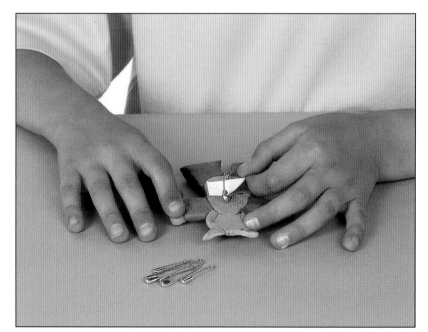

37

Starry Pot

This pot is made from slabs of drying material. The slabs are joined by smoothing the seams using a sculpting tool. Bind the inside seams first. When the pot is complete, smooth the outside seams. This pot is ideal for storing small valuables. To make a nest of pots, make two more pots – one smaller and one larger than your Starry Pot.

YOU WILL NEED

Drying material
Chopping board
Tall, thick glass
Ruler
Sculpting tool
Acrylic paints in blue, yellow, green, white
Paintbrush
White glue

1 Roll a large slab of material until it is 5mm/³⁄₁₆in thick. Use the upturned glass to cut out two circles. Use the sculpting tool to cut a rectangle 26cm/10in by 4cm/1½in. Then cut a strip of material 26cm/10in by 2cm/¾in.

2 To make the lid, roll out one of the circles until it is 6mm/¼in wider than the other circle. Score around the side of the lid and press the narrow strip around the side. Gently bind the edges together.

3 Score the side of the remaining circle and carefully wrap the rectangle of material around it. Support the sides of the pot as you bind the edges together. Smooth the joins on the inside of the pot.

4 Roll out a piece of material and press an upturned glass on it to make the outline of a circle. Cut out a small circle from the remaining material, and place it in the middle of the outlined circle. Carve the Sun's rays around it.

5 Cut out the Sun and position it on the flat surface of the lid. Place the lid on the upturned glass to dry. Allow the pot and the lid to dry for 24 hours.

6 Paint the insides and outsides of the pot and lid. When they are dry, use yellow to decorate them with stars and moons. If you are interested in astrology, you could paint star signs around the side. Allow the pot and lid to dry thoroughly before applying a varnish of 8 parts white glue to 1 part water.

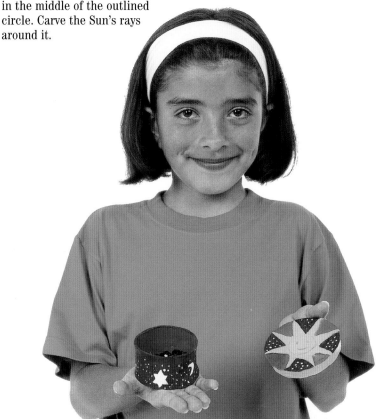

HANDY HINT

Do not forget to keep any remaining clay in a plastic bag. Seal the bag tightly so the material does not dry out. Store such materials in a cool, dark place.

Red-faced Conductor

The orchestra conductor is great
fun to make and your model is
bound to impress everyone. Is the
conductor red in the face because
he is conducting a very fast piece of
music, or is it because he is angry
with the orchestra? Maybe he is
blushing because he got one of
the notes wrong! If you like
music, try making a violinist,
a cellist or a percussionist.

YOU WILL NEED

Non-hardening plastic material in
* black, white, purple, red, blue, yellow*
Chopping board
Ruler
Sculpting tool
Cocktail stick or toothpick

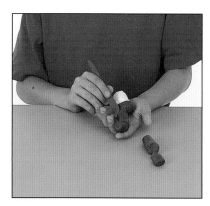

1 For the legs and feet, roll three thick sausages 5cm/2in long. Cut one in half for the feet. To make the body, roll out a black rectangle 3cm/1in by 4cm/1½in. Roll out a white rectangle the same size for the conductor's shirt. Sculpt the pieces together.

2 Roll two black sausages 3cm/1in long for the model's arms. To make the tailcoat, roll out and cut a piece of black material. The tailcoat has to be large enough to wrap halfway around the torso.

3 Cut a strip of purple material 1cm/½in by 3cm/1in. Position it to cover the join between the upper and lower body. Press on the arms and the tailcoat. Bind them to the model using your fingers.

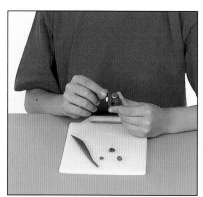

4 Roll a purple ball for the conductor's head. Press on a lump for the nose and two big red circles for cheeks. Make and position the eyes and hair. Use the tool to make the mouth.

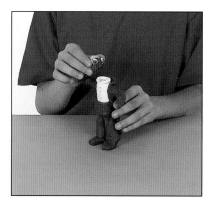

5 Make hands from two balls of purple material and press them on to the arms. Make a shirt collar from a thin snake of white material coiled into a circle. Firmly press the head into place.

6 Add black buttons and a bow tie. Ask an adult to remove the sharp ends from the stick to make a baton. Push the baton into one of the conductor's hands. Now sit back and enjoy the music!

Flowering Cactus

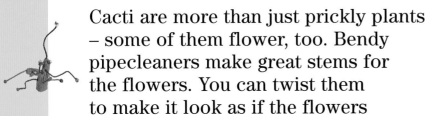

Cacti are more than just prickly plants – some of them flower, too. Bendy pipecleaners make great stems for the flowers. You can twist them to make it look as if the flowers are actually growing!

YOU WILL NEED

Non-hardening plastic material in green, red, yellow, blue
Chopping board
Ruler
Sculpting tool
Pipecleaners, in the shades of your choice

HANDY HINT

If you are unable to find pipecleaners in the shades you want, you can paint white ones using acrylic paints. Remember to cover the work surface with paper and to allow drying time.

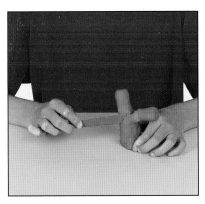

1 Roll a thick sausage of green material 5cm/2in long and 3cm/1in wide. Roll two smaller sausages 3cm/1in long and 1.5cm/½in wide. Use the sculpting tool to shape the pieces together into the form of a cactus.

2 Use the thin end of the tool to carve fine lines of different lengths into the cactus. This will make the surface of your model cactus look as prickly and as rough as the real thing.

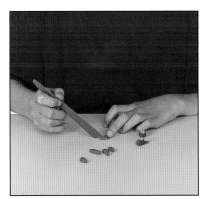

3 To make the flowers, roll tiny balls of red, yellow and blue material. Press two different shade balls together. Shape leaves from green material. Fix a leaf under each flower.

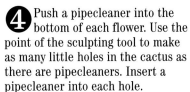

4 Push a pipecleaner into the bottom of each flower. Use the point of the sculpting tool to make as many little holes in the cactus as there are pipecleaners. Insert a pipecleaner into each hole.

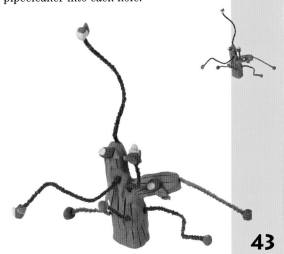

43

Supersonic Aircraft

To build a difficult model like an aircraft it is best to make it out of cardboard first. Use your imagination to create the faces of the passengers looking out of the windows.

YOU WILL NEED

Thick cardboard
Pencil
Ruler
Scissors
Masking tape
Non-hardening plastic material
in yellow, white, blue, red
Chopping board
Tall, thick glass
Sculpting tool

HANDY HINT

Remember that the length of a slit equals the width of the piece to be inserted. The width of the slit is the same as the thickness of the cardboard.

1 Draw the parts of the aircraft on to cardboard. The body should be 17cm/7in long, the wing 15cm/6in long and the tail 8cm/3in long. Draw slits on the aircraft body for the wing and the tail to slot into.

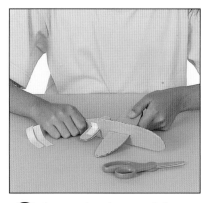

2 Cut out the pieces and the slits. Insert the wing and the tail into the slits on the body. Bind in place with masking tape. It is important that the pieces are firmly fixed and do not move.

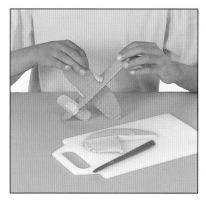

3 Roll out the yellow material using the tall glass. Cut the material into pieces. Cover one side of the cardboard structure with the yellow slabs. Do not worry if the material slabs overlap.

4 Turn the aircraft over and cover the other side with yellow slabs. Press the edges firmly together and smooth the joins.

5 Roll out white material and cut windows for both sides of the aircraft. Decorate the aircraft with blue stripes and a red nose.

Boggle-eyed Bug

Scare your friends with this horrible creepy-crawly. They will not know which way to run to escape from its boggle-eyed stare, long hairy legs and pointy teeth! You can bend the pipecleaner legs into different positions to make your minibeast wave or dance.

YOU WILL NEED

Non-hardening plastic material in purple, blue, orange, white
Chopping board
Ruler
Sculpting tool
Pipecleaners, in the shades of your choice

HANDY HINT
If you are interested in the natural world, borrow an illustrated book about insects and spiders, and make models of other minibeasts.

 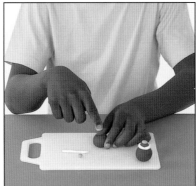 

1 In your hands, roll one ball 6cm/2½in wide from purple material to make the minibeast's body. To make a pair of bulging eyes roll two balls 3cm/1in wide from purple material.

2 Roll two small balls of blue material and press one on to each purple eyeball. Flatten two tiny balls of orange material and press one on to each blue circle. Trim the eyes with a thin snake of white material.

3 Push the thick end of the sculpting tool into the large ball. Lever it up and down to make a gaping mouth. If you do not like your first attempt, simply roll the ball in your hands and start again!

4 Press the eyes firmly into position. Add two orange nostrils. Shape a small strip of white material to make the fearsome triangular fangs. Press the fangs securely into the mouth.

5 Bend six pipecleaners to make the hairy legs. Push them into the body at even intervals to complete your creepy-crawly! To make the body look hairy, carve fine lines using the sculpting tool.

Tyrannosaurus Rex

The Tyrannosaurus Rex is back and it is living in your bedroom! This toothy dinosaur walked on its hind legs. It makes an ideal paperweight for your desk or bedside table because it is quite heavy. The Tyrannosaurus Rex is just one type of dinosaur – why not try making a pterodactyl or inventing your own fantastic reptile?

YOU WILL NEED

Non-hardening plastic material
  in green, red, yellow
Chopping board
Ruler
Sculpting tool

1 Roll five sausages of material 5cm/2in long and 2cm/1in wide for the limbs and body of the dinosaur. For the head and neck, form one lump 2cm/1in square and two smaller lumps. For the tail, roll a thick sausage 8cm/3in long and a flatter strip 5cm/2in long.

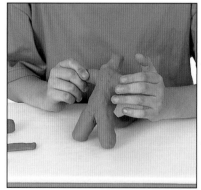

2 Bind the arms, legs, body and tail of the dinosaur together. Use one of the small lumps for a neck. Shape the two remaining lumps into a head – roll the larger one into a thick sausage and press the smaller one on top.

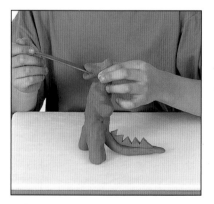

3 Use the sculping tool to carve triangles in the strip of material. Press it on to the tail. Make an opening for the mouth by levering the sculping tool up and down. Take care not to push the dinosaur's head off!

4 Roll out four thick slabs of green material to make the feet and hands of the dinosaur. Carve the pointed toes and fingers before pressing the feet and hands into position.

5 Texture the surface of the dinosaur to create scaly skin. Shape red material to make the eyes. Shape yellow material to make the teeth, the claws and the stripe down the dinosaur's back.

49

Groovy Giraffe

Giraffes have very long necks so that they can reach the juiciest and newest leaves from even the tallest trees. To make the model's neck strong, long and straight it has been made from cardboard. This is then decorated to match the rest of the body.

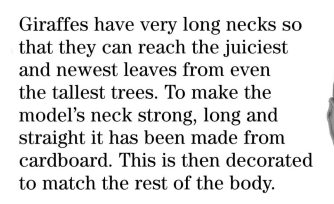

YOU WILL NEED
Non-hardening plastic material in orange, blue, black, yellow
Chopping board
Ruler
Sculpting tool
Thin yellow cardboard
Scissors
Double-sided tape

1 To make the giraffe's legs, roll four sausages 5cm/2in long and 1cm/½in wide from orange material. Then roll a sausage 9cm/3½in long and 4cm/1½in wide from orange material to make the body.

2 Bind the legs on to the body and smooth the joins. Roll a thin 9cm/3½in long snake of orange material and join the ends to make a circle. Position it where the giraffe's neck will go.

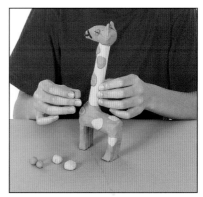

3 Cut a piece of cardboard 11cm/4½in long by 10cm/4in wide. Stick double-sided tape along one long side of it. Roll the cardboard into a tube and press the edge on to the double-sided tape.

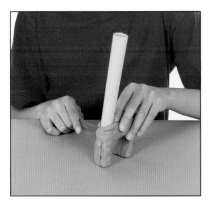

4 Push the tube through the ring of clay and into the body. Hold the tube in one hand as you bind the ring on to the tube and on to the body. If the neck is wobbly, push it further into the body.

5 To make the head, shape a ball of orange clay with your fingers. Press on two pointy ears and two blue eyes. Carve a slit in each eye to make a pupil. Roll a snake of black clay for the mouth.

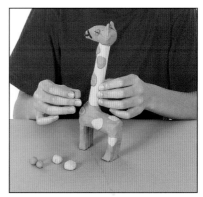

6 Push the head of the giraffe firmly on to the neck. To avoid creasing the cardboard as you do so, twist the head back and forth. Decorate the body and neck with orange and yellow dots of clay.

51

Mirror Frame

To make this terracotta-framed mirror you will need to buy a small round mirror. This carved and painted frame would make a wonderful birthday present for a friend or relative. Decorate it to match their bedroom or bathroom.

YOU WILL NEED

Terracotta drying material
Chopping board
Tall, thick glass
Small round mirror
Sculpting tool

Pastry cutter
Acrylic paints in blue, red, yellow
Paintbrush
White glue

1 Roll the terracotta material into a ball. Use the glass to roll it out into a thick circular slab. The slab needs to be larger than the mirror. To keep it circular, roll the material evenly in all directions.

2 Place the mirror in the middle of the circle of material. Make sure that it is the right way up! Push the mirror down evenly and firmly so that the terracotta material rises up around it.

3 Place the glass or any circular object that is slightly smaller than the mirror on to the middle of the mirror. Press the terracotta material over the edge of the mirror to meet the glass.

4 Roll a long snake of terracotta material and place it around the inside edge of the frame. Use the sculpting tool to trim it if it is too long. Press it gently into place with your fingertips.

5 Trim the round outer edge of the frame with the sculpting tool to make a hexagonal shape. Use the edge of the tool to decorate the inside edge of the frame with zigzag lines and patterns.

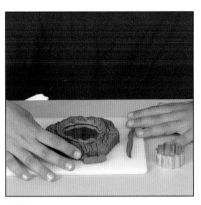
6 Form a handle and bind it on to the frame. Use a pastry cutter to make patterns in the frame. Dry for 12 hours on each side before painting. When dry, varnish with 8 parts glue diluted in 1 part water.

HANDY HINT
Make the handle for the frame as chunky as possible and press it very firmly into position. The handle needs to be able to support the weight of the mirror when it is hanging up.

53

Button Leopard

Do leopards ever change their spots? Yes, when they swap them for shiny buttons. Ask permission before you borrow buttons from the sewing box. The buttons do not have to be the same size, but small ones are easier to use than large ones.

YOU WILL NEED
Non-hardening plastic material
*   in orange, green*
Ruler
Chopping board
Buttons

54

1 Roll one large sausage 7cm/3in by 4cm/1½in and four smaller sausages in orange material to make the body and legs. Roll a ball for the head and two small balls for the ears. Roll one extra small ball.

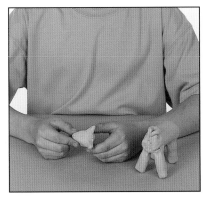

2 Press the legs into place and sculpt the joins with your fingers. Roll the extra ball to make a snake and coil it on to the body, as shown. Shape the ball to make a head. Shape and press on the ears.

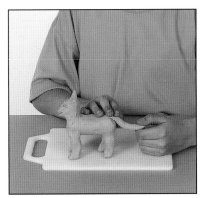

3 Bind the head on to the coil of material using your fingers. Roll a thick snake of orange material for the tail. Support the tail while you gently bind it on to the body with your fingers.

HANDY HINT

When making models of animals or humans, make the legs fairly thick and the feet large and flat. This will ensure that the model will be stable when standing.

4 Press the buttons into the leopard, spacing them out evenly. Shape two small balls of green material to make the leopard's glinting eyes. Press them into position.

Towering Skyscraper

Model skyscrapers can be any size or shade you like. They are so easy to make! Let your imagination run wild and build an entire city of them. You could even make roads using strips of black cardboard. Bring your city to life with models of people, animals and buses. Someone could be waving from the top floor of the skyscraper.

YOU WILL NEED

Non-hardening plastic material in
*   orange, yellow, blue, red, green, white*
Chopping board
Knife
Tall, thick glass
Sculpting tool

1 Roll a thick sausage of plastic material with your hands. Apply the pressure evenly so that the material is the same width all the way along.

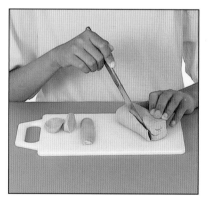

2 Use a knife to cut the top, bottom and sides off the sausage to make a rectangular block. The bottom must be flat, or the skyscraper will fall over.

3 Roll out pieces of material in different shades using the glass. Cut each piece into small squares to make the windows. Press these into position.

4 Cut a square to fit on top of the skyscraper. Press it in place. Cut two squares, both smaller than the first. Press these on to the top. Roll a thin snake of material and position as shown.

5 To make the figure leaning out of the window, shape a piece of material to make the head, arms and upper body. Use the sculpting tool to make a hole in a window.

6 Shape the bottom of the figure so that it will fit snugly into the hole. Smooth the join. Make a cat, a bird or flower-filled pot plants for other window ledges of your towering skyscraper.

Snake Pot

This pot looks like a sleeping snake curled around on itself! The technique is used in pottery and the result is called a coil pot. Use the pot to store paperclips, coins or other small items.

YOU WILL NEED

White drying material
Chopping board
Sculpting tool
Acrylic paints in yellow, red
Paintbrush
White glue

HANDY HINT

It you want to make a larger coil pot to use as a pencil holder, roll the snakes a little thicker. If you need two snakes to complete your pot, bind the snakes together and keep coiling.

1 Cut three pieces of drying material and roll each into a snake. Make the snakes as long as you can, but not too thin.

2 Tightly coil one of the snakes into a flat circle. This will be the base of the pot. If there are any gaps, gently press the coils together.

3 Build the walls of the pot by coiling a snake on top of the outer edge of the base. Smooth the ridges on the inside of the pot.

4 Continue coiling with the third snake. When you have finished, shape the end to make the face. Use the tool to mark the eyes and mouth. Decorate the edge of the pot with carved patterns.

5 Allow the pot to dry for about 12 hours on each side before painting it yellow. Allow the paint to dry before adding the spots. When dry, apply a varnish made of 8 parts white glue and 1 part water.

Grinning Cat

This grinning cat looks very pleased with itself. You can almost hear it purring! This model is very simple to make because the cat's legs are curled under its body. Do not make the tail too thin or it will break. Paint your cheery cat as brightly and boldly as possible.

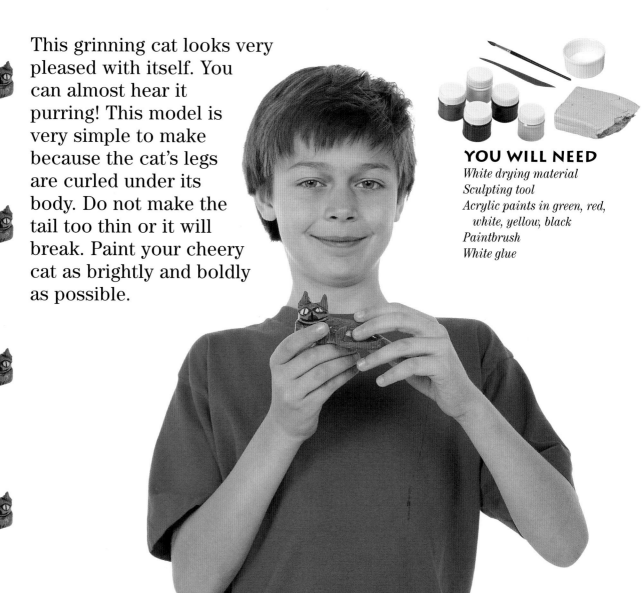

YOU WILL NEED

White drying material
Sculpting tool
Acrylic paints in green, red,
  white, yellow, black
Paintbrush
White glue

1 Roll a ball of white drying material between your palms to make the head. Then roll a thick sausage 6cm/2½in long for the cat's sleek body.

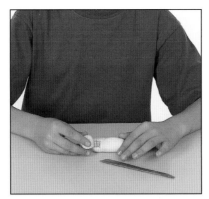

2 To fix the cat's head on to its body, score the bottom of the head with the sculpting tool and press the head firmly on to the body. Graft and smooth the join using your fingers.

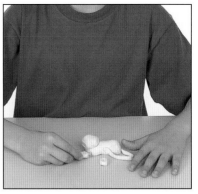
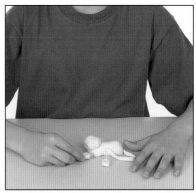

3 Cut and shape two pieces of material to make the front paws. Press them into position. Make a tail and press it on to the body. Curl the tail around the body.

4 Flatten a small piece of material with the palm of the your hand. Use the blade of the sculpting tool to carve two triangles for the cat's ears.

5 Use the tool to carve the features of the cat. You might want to try this out using a piece of leftover material. Allow the cat to dry for about 12 hours.

6 Carefully paint the cat using only the very boldest shades. Allow the paint to dry before applying a varnish made of 8 parts white glue diluted in 1 part water.

Denim Cowgirl

In the Wild West of America, cowboys and cowgirls used to round up the cattle and lasso wild horses. To do such tough work cowgirls wore high boots, denim jeans and a wide brimmed hat. This model is made from baking material that hardens when heated in the oven.

YOU WILL NEED

Baking material in brown, blue, yellow, light or dark pink
Chopping board
Sculpting tool
Baking tray

HANDY HINT

To make a lasso for the cowgirl, make a loop in one end of a short piece of wire. Form one of her hands around the other end of the wire. Shape the wire so that the loop is above her head.

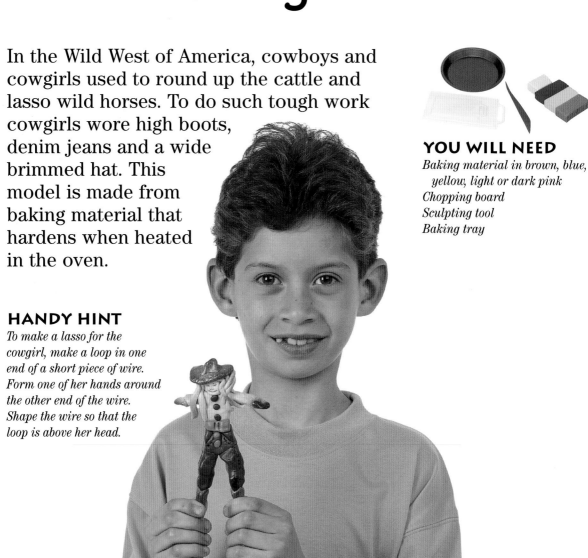

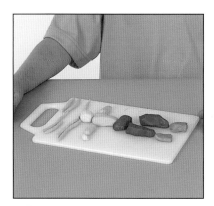

① Cut two brown pieces to make boots, three blue pieces for jeans, and three yellow pieces to make the shirt. Roll a pink ball for the head and two small balls for the hands. Roll yellow snakes for hair.

② Sculpt the main body parts together using your fingers rather than a sculpting tool. The warmth from your hands will keep the baking material soft and very easy to shape.

③ Shape the brown pieces to make a pair of high boots. Make the boots large and keep the soles of the boots flat and even. Press them on to the legs. Graft the pieces together with your fingers.

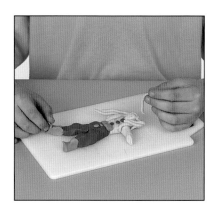

④ Roll small balls from brown and blue material and press them on to the shirt and jeans. Cut out a belt and press it on. Use the tool to mark the eyes, mouth and nose. Attach her flowing hair.

⑤ To make the brim of the hat, roll a ball in brown material and flatten it. Roll another small ball and shape it to make the crown of the hat. Press it on. Shape the brim so that the hat looks old.

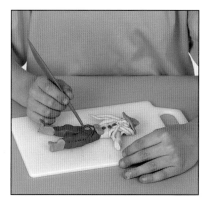

⑥ Make marks down the legs of the jeans to imitate the stitching. Gently lay the model on a baking tray. Ask an adult to bake it in the oven according to the instructions on the packet.

ACKNOWLEDGEMENTS

We would like to thank the following children for appearing in this book:

Mohammed Adil Ali Ahmed
Steve Aristizabal
Holly Everett
George Georgiev
Briony Irwin
Kayode Irwin
Victoria Lebedeva
Kerry Morgan
Jamie Rosso
Nida Sayeed
Catherine Tolstoy

Gratitude also to their parents and Hampden Gurney School.